Accepted in the Beloved

Yizu Berhe.

The House of Prisca and Aquila

OUR MISSION AT THE HOUSE OF PRISCA AND AQUILA IS TO PRODUCE QUALITY books that expound accurately the word of God to empower women and men to minister together in a multicultural church. Our writers have a positive view of the Bible as God's revelation that affects both thoughts and words, so it is plenary, historically accurate, and consistent in itself; fully reliable; and authoritative as God's revelation. Because God is true, God's revelation is true, inclusive to men and women and speaking to a multicultural church, wherein all the diversity of the church is represented within the parameters of egalitarianism and inerrancy.

The word of God is what we are expounding, thereby empowering women and men to minister together in all levels of the church and home. The reason we say women and men together is because that is the model of Prisca and Aquila, ministering together to another member of the church—Apollos: "Having heard Apollos, Priscilla and Aquila took him aside and more accurately expounded to him the Way of God" (Acts 18:26). True exposition, like true religion, is by no means boring—it is fascinating. Books that reveal and expound God's true nature "burn within us" as they elucidate the Scripture and apply it to our lives.

This was the experience of the disciples who heard Jesus on the road to Emmaus: "Were not our hearts burning while Jesus was talking to us on the road, while he was opening the scriptures to us?" (Luke 24:32). We are hoping to create the classics of tomorrow: significant and accessible trade and academic books that "burn within us."

Our "house" is like the home to which Prisca and Aquila no doubt brought Apollos as they took him aside. It is like the home in Emmaus where Jesus stopped to break bread and reveal his presence. It is like the house built on the rock of obedience to Jesus (Matt 7:24). Our "house," as a euphemism for our publishing team, is a home where truth is shared and Jesus' Spirit breaks bread with us, nourishing all of us with his bounty of truth.

We are delighted to work together with Wipf and Stock in this series and welcome submissions on a wide variety of topics from an egalitarian inerrantist global perspective. The House of Prisca and Aquila is also a ministry center affiliated with the International Council of Community Churches.

For more information, visit www.houseofpriscaandaquila.com.

Accepted in the Beloved

A Devotional Bible Study for Women
on Finding Healing and Wholeness in God's Love

LESLIE ANN MCKINNEY

WIPF & STOCK · Eugene, Oregon

ACCEPTED IN THE BELOVED
A Devotional Bible Study for Women on Finding Healing and Wholeness in God's Love

House of Prisca and Aquila Series

ISBN 13: 978-1-55635-936-1

Manufactured in the U.S.A.

 © Robert Milek / 123RF

To All God's Daughters

May you come to know and experience for yourselves the depth
of God's unconditional love and acceptance. (Ephesians 3:15–17)

In Loving Memory of my husband,
Rutherford Hayes McKinney

Contents

Acknowledgements

THE LORD GAVE ME the desire to write *Accepted in the Beloved* and granted me the grace, perseverance, and wisdom to finish the task. God's unending goodness and incredible love never cease to amaze me. For her constant critique, care, listening ear, and hours of time, I am immensely thankful to Karen Smith, my dear seminary friend and sister in the Lord. She is graced with wisdom, gentle with criticism, and a faithful follower of Jesus Christ. I am grateful to Aída Besançon Spencer, mentor, ministry colleague, and friend, for her exemplary scholarship, constant encouragement, and hours of editing. Her profession of teaching women to exegete properly the word of truth and of training and encouraging women to lead has transformed my life. For her passion for teaching, encouraging, and preparing women leaders in the church, and for offering women the opportunity to pursue their dreams and fulfill their callings in Christ, I am thankful and indebted to Alice P. Mathews. For her hours of time, her expert editing skills, and her thoughtful critique of my work, I am thankful to Deb Beatty Mel. Her calming spirit and peace-filled heart have encouraged me to keep moving forward with steadiness and persistence. Finally, I am grateful to my husband, Hayes McKinney, for his love, support, and willingness to let me follow God's lead in my life, enabling me to pursue my studies over these last years.

About This Study

THE BIBLE STUDY *ACCEPTED in the Beloved* is based on Ephesians 1:6, which says, "To the praise of his glorious grace in which he has made us accepted in the beloved" (Webster Bible). *Accepted in the Beloved* is written for all of God's daughters who have suffered any form of abuse and who long to know and experience the intimate love and acceptance of God.

The study includes six topical lessons, one for each of six weeks, written to encourage healing, growth, and transformation. Each of the six weekly lessons includes three different sections: Learning God's Truth, Experiencing God, and Sharing God's Love. Learning God's Truth is designed to take you through a study of God's word in order to enlighten your minds to God's truth. The second section, Experiencing God, is designed to help you grow through contemplative exercises in order to foster deeper heart knowledge of God's truth and spiritual transformation. Sharing God's Love, the third section, is designed to encourage you to reach out beyond yourself as you apply what you have learned. A rose, a symbol of God's love, is placed throughout each lesson of the study to indicate a break in the study and to provide time to reflect in your journal any thoughts or feelings that arise during the exercises or in response to the questions.

INDIVIDUAL PARTICIPATION

As with anything, the more you put into the study, the more you will gain. As you participate in the study, it is important to practice three important principles.

Pray without ceasing

Make prayer a critical part of this study and your healing journey. Ask God to guide you as you seek to learn and be transformed by God's truth. If possible, additionally engage others to pray for you during the six-week period, because prayer is powerful and can be an important key to unlocking the doors to your emotional and spiritual freedom. Pray for strength, healing, growth, transformation, a deeper revelation of God's love and acceptance, and for God to lead and guide you each day as you read and study God's word, as you experience God through practicing the contemplative exercises, and as you reach out to others in need.

Be diligent in study

The word of God is powerful and will bring life-renewing changes as you read, study, and apply it to your everyday life. Please take as much time as you need to study God's truth and answer the questions. Doing the necessary work will benefit you greatly in the end. Remember, healing takes time, so be gentle with yourself and stay faithful to the process.

Reflect through journaling and contemplation

It is recommended that you keep a separate journal as you work through this bible study, to record any important and powerful thoughts, feelings, and reflections Journaling opens the door to healing as it allows you to process unwanted emotions and feelings. Sometimes, as you commit to writing, the floodgates of your heart open up, unleashing pent-up feelings and emotions that you never knew existed. Let your thoughts flow unhindered and try not to worry about your grammar or punctuation. This exercise is not about perfection, but rather about healing and wholeness. Allow God to minister to you as you journal and practice the contemplative exercises. Spending time in quiet and solitude will allow God to minister to you deeply and eventually free you to be the woman God created you to be as you fulfill God's purposes for your life.

SMALL GROUP PARTICIPATION AND LEADER'S TIPS

After you complete your weekly lesson, you will meet once a week (or bi-weekly if that works better) for group discussion, sharing, questions, and prayer. Small group participation can help solidify God's truth in your heart and mind, allow you the space to be yourself, and provide the opportunity to experience authentic Christian community.

About the Leader

The woman who leads the group should have past experience in leading small groups and feel called of God to encourage healing and wholeness in others. She should be a woman of faith who is sensitive, loving, a good listener, prayerful, and a servant leader.

Tips for the Leader

It is important if you are meeting in a weekly (or bi-weekly) group that you keep the group open to receiving new members for two consecutive weeks only. After the second group meeting, it is wise to close the group to new members in order for the group to grow in developing trust, cohesiveness, and safe intimate sharing. It is also important for each participant to have experienced a certain measure of inner healing in her heart and life in order to gain the most out of the material and contemplative exercises.

When you meet as a group, it is not necessary to go over every question and answer for each lesson, but only the highlights. Pick several questions for each lesson and ask the women to share their answers. The goal is for the women to understand the topic or theme of each lesson and apply what they are learning to their lives. Be creative as you lead; be open to God as God leads through you. Pray before you begin each meeting.

Tips for Group Members

If possible, practice three key principles as you gather together.

Be true to yourself

Honesty and openness create intimacy with God and others. When you have suffered abuse, trust takes time to develop. A safe and loving group will enable you to be yourself as you begin to share from your heart. Stay true to your thoughts and feelings as you express them within the group. This is one place where you do not have to be perfect in order to be loved and accepted—just be yourself. You may be pleasantly surprised when God uses this group experience to help you understand yourself better through the lives of others.

Give others space to share their stories

Sharing your story as you answer questions and participate within the group is important. In fact, it is so important that God created space within this group for you to be able to share openly and freely. It is also important for others to be able to share their stories with you. Try to be considerate of others' needs to share—your intentional love, care, time, and active listening will encourage healing in others. One of the most powerful means of healing is through community.

Patiently wait on God for your healing

The healing process takes time. Learn to be gentle, patient, and loving with yourself as you participate in this Bible study and small group. God is capable of miraculously healing anyone, but, often, God chooses to heal over time. When you wait on God for your healing, amazing things can happen. You can get to know yourself better, and you can become more acquainted with God and his gracious and loving ways. These are two good reasons to continue to wait on God's timing for your healing.

Suggested Questions for the Leader for Each Lesson

1. What would you most like to get out of this Bible study? (This is for lesson 1 only, to understand where people are on their journey of healing.)

2. How did the Learning God's Truth section go for you? What did you learn? How do you need to grow? Which question might you like to share?

3. What were some important truths you learned?

4. Do you have any questions about the material studied?

5. How was the Experiencing God exercise for you? Share your thoughts and experiences.

6. Did God speak to your heart? What did God say to you? What may God want you to learn?

7. Was the Experiencing God exercise a freeing experience for you? Please share.

8. Were you able to practice reaching out to someone this week? If so, how did this go for you?

Close by praying for all members. Be open to God's leading, and, if others are open, have them pray for one another.

May you enjoy the study as you work through painful life experiences. May you grow in the knowledge of God's amazing love and acceptance. You are so worth the time and effort because you are uniquely created in the image of God!

Chosen in Love

A S WE BEGIN OUR study together, allow me to share a personal childhood story with you. When I was a small child, I owned a doll named Betty. Betty was special to me; she was my favorite doll. Betty was beautiful, with long, dark, thick hair, and wide brown eyes. I loved to spend time playing with Betty. In fact, I played with her so often that poor Betty started wearing out. Betty lost an arm, and then, eventually, one of her legs was missing, and at one point, I cut Betty's hair all off. Poor Betty! To many, she was a terrible sight, but not to me. I loved her no matter what she looked like.

Unfortunately, my mother did not share the same sentiments. One morning when I awoke, I could not find Betty. I looked in my bed, under the covers, on the floor, and under the bed. I looked everywhere I could think of, but Betty was missing. I asked my mother where Betty was, and she said, "Betty is outside in the garage in the trash can where she belongs. I threw her away. She was all ragged and worn. You don't want that old doll Betty anymore, do you?"

"You threw her away?" I cried. "That's my doll!" Then the thought occurred to me that I could still rescue her before she ended up at the dump. Hastily, I slipped outside, pajamas and all, and rummaged through the trash cans until I spotted her head sticking out of one of the cans. "There you are, Betty," I said. I rescued her out of the trash can, brushed the dirt off, and held her close to me. I felt relieved and pleased with Betty back in my arms.

In my Doctor of Ministry class in 2002, as we discussed body image, women's self-esteem, and the impact that playing with a Barbie doll had on children's development, I was reminded of Betty. Suddenly, I realized that Betty had far more meaning and significance in my life than I had ever imagined. The story of Betty was a divine call from God to help his beloved daughters, especially those who have been broken and wounded through the pain of abuse, to know and experience God's unconditional love and acceptance.

I pray that you will come to experience God's amazing unconditional love and acceptance like never before. Is this not what the Gospel message is all about?

As you consider this story, can you identify with it in any way? Write your thoughts on the lines below.

_____

_____

_____

_____

Perhaps you have felt rejected, broken, or like a throwaway.

Do you really believe that God loves and accepts you?

Do you believe that you have to be perfect and whole in order to be loved and acceptable to God?

Have you ever struggled with believing that God really loves you?

If you have, you are not alone. Many people struggle with believing this profound truth for various reasons.

Maybe, when you were a child, your parents were unable to nurture and accept you the way you needed them to, and this has hindered you from experiencing the reality of God's unconditional love. Perhaps you have experienced repeated rejection or abuse from your spouse, a close friend, or a significant other, and this has hindered you from believing that you are precious, valuable, and fully acceptable to God. Maybe you struggle daily with some temptation or addictive behavior, and you do not believe that God could possibly love and accept you. Instead, you imagine God's rejection of you, and you believe that, in order for God to accept you, you have to be perfect!

Whatever your background, do you long to know and experience the intimate love and acceptance of God? Would it not be wonderfully freeing to wake up every morning, knowing beyond a doubt just how much God loves and accepts you? This would be life-transforming, would it not? This is a hard kernel of truth to understand and internalize. However, let us look at God's word together and discover the amazing truth about God's love and acceptance.

My prayer for you is that, over the next six weeks, as you embark on this exciting journey of learning and growing in God's word, that you will experience the intimate love and acceptance of God—maybe the love and acceptance that you have longed for your whole life long. May this truth transform your life and cause you to grow in a more intimate relationship with God.

Before you begin this week's Bible study, take a moment and ask God to guide you as you study his word and to bring revelation to your mind and heart about his life-transforming truths.

LEARNING GOD'S TRUTH

In lesson 1, we will study Scripture passages 1 John 4:7–8, 1:4–9; John 3:16; Ephesians 1:1–10; Romans 8:35–39; and Revelation 7:14.

> [7]Beloved, let us love one another, because love is from God; everyone who loves is born of God and knows God. [8]Whoever does not love does not know God, for God is love. (1 John 4:7–8)

> [4]We are writing these things so that our joy may be complete. [5] This is the message we have heard from him and proclaim to you, that God is light and in him there is no darkness at all. [6]If we say that we have fellowship with him while we are walking in darkness, we lie and do not do what is true; [7]but if we walk in the light as he himself is in the light, we have fellowship with one another, and the blood of Jesus his Son cleanses us from all sin. [8]If we say that we have no sin, we deceive ourselves, and the truth is not in us. [9]If we confess our sins, he who is faithful and just will forgive us our sins and cleanse us from all unrighteousness. (1 John 1:4–9)

> For God so loved the world that he gave his only Son, so that everyone who believes in him may not perish, but may have eternal life. (John 3:16)

God is _____ .
What does this mean to you?

_____

_____

How did God show his love for you? _____ .

What an amazing gift of sacrificial love! God loves you deeply; there is no greater expression of love than for one to lay down his life for you. Jesus died for you; if you were the only person on the face of the earth, Jesus would have died for you.

Why did Jesus have to die? _____

By faith, when you confess your sins, you are saved. Because God's very nature is love, what is God's command to us?

This sounds easy, but it is not always so easy to love others. Now, you might be thinking, "Well, I try to love, but it is not easy. I have been so mistreated by those who were supposed to love and nurture me that I have a very difficult time loving others."

This is quite human and understandable. It is very difficult to love others when you have not received love from your significant others. You cannot give out of an empty vessel. This is precisely why you need to soak in the unconditional love of God before you can attempt to love others. It is all right to give yourself permission to take time to grow in the love of God before you attempt to love others unconditionally, especially those who have harmed and hurt you deeply. Be gentle with yourself. Furthermore, love comes from God, and we can only love with *agapē* love, a selfless, sacrificial love, when we allow Christ's love to flow through us to others.

What circumstances in your life have hindered you from knowing and experiencing God's love?

Either journal your thoughts and feelings or share your heart with others in the group.

How have these negative life experiences affected the way you image God? Take a few moments and write down how you have imaged God because of the experiences of others.

Who is God to you? _____

Coming to know and experience a loving God is a process. It takes time to grow in the wisdom and knowledge of God, it takes time to heal the memories and it takes time to trust a God whom you cannot see.

Now, let us turn to the book of Ephesians.

¹Paul, an apostle of Christ Jesus by the will of God, To the saints who are in Ephesus and are faithful in Christ Jesus: ²Grace to you and peace from God our Father and the Lord Jesus Christ. ³Blessed be the God and Father of our Lord Jesus Christ, who has blessed us in Christ with every spiritual blessing in the heavenly places, ⁴just as he chose us in Christ before the foundation of the world to be holy and blameless before him in love. ⁵He destined us for adoption as his children through Jesus Christ, according to the good pleasure of his will, ⁶to the praise of his glorious grace that he freely bestowed on us in the Beloved. ⁷In him we have redemption through his blood, the forgiveness of our trespasses, according to the riches of his grace ⁸that he lavished on us. With all wisdom and insight ⁹he has made known to us the mystery of his will, according to his good pleasure that he set forth in Christ, ¹⁰as a plan for the fullness of time, to gather up all things in him, things in heaven and things on earth. (Eph 1:1–10)

The apostle Paul originally wrote this letter to the faithful saints of Ephesus while he was in prison. His purpose in writing to the church at Ephesus was to encourage the community in the faith among both Jews and Gentiles and to help the body of Christ to live in peace and love with one another. But in order for believers to live in true peace and love, each must first know his and her identity in Christ. Each person must know who he or she is in relation to Jesus Christ and understand this new life in Christ.

The apostle Paul tells us that, as God's beloved children, we have been blessed in Christ with every spiritual blessing.

To whom do we belong? _Christ_ Yes, we belong to Christ.

What are the spiritual blessings that God has blessed us with in Christ?

Name three of these spiritual blessings that you learned about in Ephesians 1:1–10:

1) _to be holy and blameless before him in love_ (v. 4)
2) _he destined us for adoption as his children_ (v. 5)
3) _to gather up all things in him, in heaven & earth._ (v. 10)

We have received the past blessing of being "chosen" in Christ before the foundations of the world. You became a part of God's family when you came to believe in Jesus Christ, a global family both here on the earth and in heaven. You do not stand alone. You were chosen by your loving God, called out for his divine purposes and for his good pleasure. What a privilege! What a calling! You are his children through Jesus Christ, accepted in the Beloved. As children, you are still growing and learning, still in process. Although you have not yet arrived, you are still working together as a community on the way to perfection in Christ. Just reflect on this truth: You were chosen in Christ before you were even born. God knew that you would exist one day and be his beloved child. You have always been precious to him even before you existed.

What does it mean that you were chosen before the foundations of the world?

And what were you chosen for? Read verse 4.

Imagine God chose you in love to be holy and blameless before him—an awesome privilege, but a grave responsibility.

The second spiritual blessing is that God adopted you as his daughter through Jesus Christ according to God's good pleasure. God took great joy in planning beforehand to adopt you into his family and grant you freedom from your sins through the blood of Christ.

What does it mean that you were adopted by God? Why did you need to be adopted?

The fact that you came to faith in Christ is an act of God's divine grace. Grace is God's unmerited favor that he bestowed on you in the Beloved. You have been accepted in the Beloved just as you are; you did not have to earn this love or acceptance. God welcomed you with open arms into his family. You are no longer alone. You no longer have to suffer alone; you have been made holy and blameless in Christ Jesus, and you are adopted into the glorious family of your Beloved. What a great blessing! Thank God for his blessing to you.

And the third blessing is the future promise of being united with all of God's children throughout the ages.[1] One day, when the fullness of time has arrived, God will gather up all things in him, things in heaven and things on earth. God's people will gather from every tribe, language, and nation before God's throne to love and worship our Beloved for all

1. John R.W. Stott, *The Message of Ephesians* (Downers Grove, Ill.: InterVarsity, 1979), 41.

eternity. What a privilege to be a part of the family of God! When the fullness of the age arrives, all our hardships in this earthly life will seem momentary in comparison to meeting our glorious Lord arrayed in full splendor and being in his presence for all eternity. Take a moment to reflect on what this will be like.

Let us take a look at another passage that will help us to understand God's amazing love. Please read Romans 8:35–39 and see that, no matter what we go through in this earthly life, that we are never separated from Christ's love.

> 35Who will separate us from the love of Christ? Will hardship, or distress, or persecution, or famine, or nakedness, or peril, or sword? 36As it is written, "For your sake we are being killed all day long; we are accounted as sheep to be slaughtered." 37No, in all these things we are more than conquerors through him who loved us. 38For I am convinced that neither death, nor life, nor angels, nor rulers, nor things present, nor things to come, nor powers, 39nor height, nor depth, nor anything else in all creation, will be able to separate us from the love of God in Christ Jesus our Lord.

Because of the nature of your past circumstances, there may have been times in your life when you have experienced feelings of abandonment, perhaps even from those who were supposed to love and support you the most. We live in a fallen world, and, unfortunately, evil happens. People hurt us, abandon us, abuse us, misunderstand us, and ignore our deepest needs. Those we should have been able to depend on have let us down. However, the word tells us that God has always been there and promises never to leave us. (The word "separate" in this context means to "go away" or "depart."[2])

What are the seven forms of suffering Paul mentions in this passage? (v. 35)

hardship, distress, persecution, famine, nakedness, peril, sword,

Paul says none of these problems in life will ever separate us from the love of Christ. Share what this means to you.

_____

_____

2. Joseph H. Thayer, *Thayer's Greek-English Lexicon of the New Testament* (Peabody, Mass.: Hendrickson Publishers, 2003), 674.

The Roman citizens were serving God with all their strength, sacrificing themselves for Christ's sake. They experienced everything Paul mentions, and, as a minister of Christ, Paul did as well. (Read 2 Corinthians 11:22–32 to see some of what Paul went through as he served the Lord.)

Not only do the problems of life not separate us from Christ's love, but Paul also tells us that nothing shall ever separate us from Christ's love.

What else does Paul mention that he is convinced shall never separate us, God's children, from God's love? (Rom 35–39).

_____

_____

Paul says that not even death shall separate us from God's love. How awesome is God's love for us! If we know Jesus, we never have to fear God leaving us or abandoning us. We can then put our complete trust and confidence in God, for, although others may have let us down, God never will. What about sin? Does sin separate us from God? Even sin never separates us from God's love, yet it will indeed affect our fellowship. But if we confess our sins daily, we will remain in love.

> 4We are writing these things so that our joy may be complete. 5This is the message we have heard from him and proclaim to you, that God is light and in him there is no darkness at all. 6If we say that we have fellowship with him while we are walking in darkness, we lie and do not do what is true; 7but if we walk in the light as he himself is in the light, we have fellowship with one another, and the blood of Jesus his Son cleanses us from all sin. 8If we say that we have no sin, we deceive ourselves, and the truth is not in us. 9If we confess our sins, he who is faithful and just will forgive us our sins and cleanse us from all unrighteousness. (1 John 1:4–9)

Read also Revelation 17:14 and Romans 8:37.

> They will make war on the Lamb, and the Lamb will conquer them, for he is Lord of lords and King of kings, and those with him are called and chosen and faithful. (Rev 17:14)

> No, in all these things we are more than conquerors through him who loved us. (Rom 8:37)

What is a conqueror? _____

The word meaning, "conquer" in Greek *(hupernikaō)* has a prefix attached to it. The prefix *huper* means "above" or "surpassing," which means that we will not only conquer, but we will be *super*-victorious as we live out our faith in Christ.[3]

How will you conquer? As you continue to walk by faith, one day at a time, with God's strength, you will not only overcome all the evil that was perpetrated against you, but through Christ, you will also overcome the world! You are loved with an everlasting love, and you have significant meaning and purpose for life.

Message of Love

Before we move on to the Experiencing God section, I want to reiterate a truth you just studied. You are deeply loved! In fact, you are so loved that God gave up his only Son so that everyone who believes may not perish but have everlasting life! That is right, Jesus died for you!

> And if you confess with your lips Jesus is Lord and believe in you heart that God raised him from the dead, you will be saved. (Rom 10:9)

The Gospel is a message of amazing love! If you so desire, take a few moments in prayer asking God to forgive you for your sins and to come into your heart so you can have assurance of eternal life.

EXPERIENCING GOD

It is one thing to know in your head that God loves you. It is yet another thing to know deep within your heart. As the old saying goes, the longest road is the road from your head to your heart. This is why it is important to practice the spiritual disciplines in order to experience the deep love of God. In my own life, the greatest tool that God has used to grow me in his love is simply being with him in silence and solitude.

Sit in a comfortable, relaxed position. Breathe in deeply and then breathe out. Do this three or four times. Spend a few minutes in prayer thanking God for his amazing love for you and for enabling you to know and experience his love more intimately. Pray that God would set your mind free from any distorted image of God and that you will continue to grow in the knowledge that God—who is love—is approachable, intimate, compassionate, and comforting, and that God desires to be with you now and every day for the rest of your life.

3. Ibid., 641.

Then, as you rest in God, meditate on Ephesians 3:14–21. (Meditate means to read very slowly and prayerfully, chewing on each word and allowing room for the Holy Spirit to speak.) Ask the Holy Spirit to guide you as you read the passage. Pay attention to any word or phrase that may strike you. What is God saying to you through his word? Read this passage a second time, and, this time, ask God what he wants you to learn from his word. Reflect on what you learned and journal your thoughts.

In my own prayer life, I continue to pray this prayer daily for my life and the life of the church. I have found that praying the word of God is powerful and effective, and, of course, God's word never returns void (Isa 55:11).

> For this reason I bow my knees before the Father, from whom every family in heaven and on earth takes its name. I pray that, according to the riches of his glory, he may grant that you may be strengthened in your inner being with power through his Spirit, and that Christ may dwell in your hearts through faith, as you are being rooted and grounded in love. I pray that you may have the power to comprehend, with all the saints, what is the breadth and length and height and depth, and to know the love of Christ that surpasses knowledge, so that you may be filled with all the fullness of God. Now to him who by the power at work within us is able to accomplish abundantly far more than all we can ask or imagine, to him be glory in the church and in Christ Jesus to all generations, forever and ever. Amen. (Eph 3:14–21)

SHARING GOD'S LOVE

Reach out in love today to one person who needs to experience more of God's love. Do something for him or her that will show the love of Christ. Spend time listening to that person, write an encouraging note or email, or be open to however God may lead you. Share how it went for you.

You are finished with lesson one. Great job! In the next lesson you will study the topic "My Image, a Reflection of God." You will learn some amazing truths about who you are as a precious child of God!

My Image, a Reflection of God

I N OUR FIRST LESSON, we learned that God unconditionally loves and accepts us. The spiritual magnitude of this truth is mind-boggling. The God of the whole universe deems us valuable and worthy to receive his gift of love. Now, although we know this in our heads, it is incredibly difficult to believe this deep down in our hearts. We just cannot believe that we are valuable and worthy of God's love; therefore, many survivors of abuse suffer from a poor self-image.

What is self-image? Self-image is simply the conception one has of one's self and the assessment of one's personal worth.[1] When we suffer any form of abuse or maltreatment by others, oftentimes our self-image is damaged. The people who abused us acted as a mirror—a distorted mirror—reflecting false messages about who we are as children of God. These distorted images affect the way we feel and think about ourselves, and they also affect our relationships to God and others. The truth is that the image that has been mirrored back to us is not who we are.[2] Who we are is who God created us to be. Have you ever actually wondered, "Who am I?"

If so, you are not alone. Many of us have been searching for the answer to this question our whole lives. If you were mistreated or abused in any way when you were growing up, you might have developed a people-pleasing personality in an attempt to gain the love and acceptance you never received, but still long for. When you live to please others, you sacrifice who you really are, who God created you to be. And what you develop is what is known as an adaptive or false self, a self who is not true

---

1. *Dictionary.com*, n.p. [cited 15 October 2005]. Online: www.dicionary.com.

2. Carroll Saussy, *God Images and Self Esteem: Empowering Women in a Patriarchal Society* (Louisville: Westminister/John Knox, 1991), 32.

to your own feelings, emotions, thoughts, wants, or needs.[3] You live to fulfill the expectations of others. You must learn to live out of your true self. This is why this lesson is focused on learning about who God created you to be, so you can be free to be yourself—free to become the woman God intended you to be.

What thoughts come to your mind when you think about yourself?

_____

_____

_____

_____

Who are you according to God's truth? Today let us start from the beginning in Genesis 1:26–27, 31, and then we will look at other passages—Psalm 139:13–16; Ephesians 2:10, and Romans 8:14–17.

LEARNING GOD'S TRUTH

In Genesis 1:26–27, 31 we read:

> [26]Then God said, "Let us make humankind in our image, according to our likeness; and let them have dominion over the fish of the sea, and over the birds of the air, and over the cattle, and over all the wild animals of the earth, and over every creeping thing that creeps upon the earth." [27]So God created humankind in his image, in the image of God he created them; male and female he created them. . . . [31]God saw everything that he had made, and indeed, it was very good.

Please fill in the blanks for verse 26.
God said, "Let _____ make humankind in _____ image, according to _____ likeness."

Who do you think God is referring to when he says "us" or "our"?

_____

Amazing! From the very beginning, we see the triune God—the Father, Son, and Holy Spirit—working together to create humankind. And we are created in the very image of the triune God. Is that not the

3. Ibid., 33.

most amazing reality? And not only that, but both male and female were created equal by God. There is no hierarchy in God's creation of humankind. We are all one, and we have been stamped with the very image and likeness of God.

What do you think it means that God created you in God's image and likeness?

_____

_____

In what way do you resemble God, or what attributes of God do you reflect?

_____

_____

What attributes would you like to reflect?

_____

_____

Share how it makes you feel that God created you in his very own image and likeness.

_____

_____

What is the one adjective that describes God's creation? (v. 31).

_____

How do you see yourself?

_____

_____

How would you like to see yourself?

_____

_____

Please take a few minutes to pray. Ask God to help you to see yourself the way God sees you. Continue in prayer as the Lord leads.

Now let us turn to Psalm 139:13–16.

> ^{13}For it was you who formed my inward parts; you knit me together in my mother's womb. ^{14}I praise you, for I am fearfully and wonderfully made. Wonderful are your works; that I know very well. ^{15}My frame was not hidden from you, when I was being made in secret, intricately woven in the depths of the earth. ^{16}Your eyes beheld my unformed substance. In your book were written all the days that were formed for me, when none of them as yet existed.

Name the two adjectives that describe how God made you (v. 14).

1) _____

2) _____

Do you believe this about yourself? _____

If not, what would it take for you to believe this truth?

_____

_____

Did it ever occur to you that God knew you before he created you? Do you believe that God created you because he loves you so and has special plans and purposes for you?

You are an amazing creation, uniquely designed and intricately formed and knit together. God's eyes beheld your unformed substance. This means that God knew you and loved you before you came into being, and knows all the days that were formed for you. Imagine! God knew you before you were born and knows how your life will unfold according to his divinely ordained plans for you. You are precious to God!

Reflect on your thoughts and feelings about what you mean to God.

Let us now turn to the Ephesians passage.

> For we are what he has made us, created in Christ Jesus for good works, which God prepared beforehand to be our way of life. (Eph 2:10)

From your mother's womb, God created you in his image and likeness and he saw you, his creation, as good! Now in your new birth, as a believer in Christ, what is God's desire for your life?

What do you believe is God's unique desire for you?

_____

_____

To what vocation has God called you or might God be calling you?

_____

_____

    Take a few minutes now to thank God for creating you. Pray that God will fulfill his purposes in your life and that God will use all you have gone through to bless and glorify his name.

    Let us end this week's study by reading Romans 8:14–17.

> 14For all who are led by the Spirit of God are children of God. 15For you did not receive a spirit of slavery to fall back into fear, but you have received a spirit of adoption. When we cry, "Abba! Father!" 16it is that very Spirit bearing witness with our spirit that we are children of God, 17and if children, then heirs, heirs of God and joint heirs with Christ—if, in fact, we suffer with him so that we may also be glorified with him.

How do you know that you are a child of God (v.16)?

_____

    You can have full and complete confidence that you are a child of God because God's Spirit bears witness to your spirit.

In addition to being a child of God, what other privileges do you have in relationship to God?

_____

_____

    What does this mean that you are God's heir and a joint heir with Christ? Do you understand the magnitude of this? What is your responsibility before God? What rich relationships you have with the triune God! You not only belong to God as his child, but you are also an heir of God and a joint heir with Christ. Wow! What a privilege to belong to God's family.

Share your thoughts on what it means for you to belong to the family of God.

_____

_____

After working through this week's lesson, "My Image, a Reflection of God's Image," please take a few minutes and answer the question "Who am I?" by making an "I am" list.[4] Make the list as long as you want. Place the phrase "I am" at the top of a blank page and list all those "I ams" that describe you as God's child. For instance, you might say, "I am a child of God," "I am loved," "I am faithful," or "I am a teacher"—whatever comes to your heart and mind.

EXPERIENCING GOD

Choose one of these two exercises, or if you have time enjoy both.

Mirror Exercise

Approximately 20 minutes: "Your image, a reflection of God's image."[5]

Sit or stand about two feet from a mirror. Gaze into the mirror looking for Christ in you. Try to look beyond your eyes into the person God created you to be.

What do you see?

Do you see pain? Do you see love? Do you see sadness? Do you see life?

Allow the Holy Spirit to speak to you as you look at yourself. Ask the Lord to help you see yourself the way God sees you. Pray for guidance and the desire to surrender to whatever comes to you.

Who are you? What thoughts, feelings or emotions arise?

Is this comfortable? Uncomfortable? What is God saying to you?

Allow your thoughts and feelings to flow; do not hinder the work of the Spirit.

4. The idea of the "I am" list came from a special friend, Theresa Piacentini. Theresa went to be with the Lord on April 28, 2005.

5. The mirror exercise came from a spiritual directors' group training help at the Free Christian Church in Andover, Mass., in 2005, taught by Andrea Lerman. This exercise comes from the book *Living in the Presence* by Tilden Edwards (New York: Harper Collins, 1995) and is found in chapter 4, "Suspending the Interior Observer," on pages 58–60.

When you are done, take some time to journal your reflections.

The purpose of this exercise is to see beyond your appearance into the person God created you to be. Hopefully, this exercise will help you grow in loving yourself and loving others, as you also try to look beyond others' appearances and see Christ in them.

Contemplative Exercise

Sit in a comfortable, relaxed position, and allow yourself to rest in Christ. Spend five minutes in solitude and silence in God's presence. After five minutes, allow God to speak to you.

What is God saying? What is God trying to communicate to you? Does he want you to know how loved you are? Does God want you to understand how important you are to him? What Scripture, if any, comes to mind?

Respond to God. Share your heart with him. Tell him how you truly feel, and be as open and candid as you desire. God desires your openness and honesty. Tell God what you need and pray that he will meet this need.

When you are finished, if you are doing this as a group, take a few minutes to share the thoughts and feelings of your experience with others. Allow them to affirm you. If you are alone, spend some time journaling your reflections of this time with God. Did you enjoy it? Did you feel safe with God? Did you sense God's presence? Allow your thoughts and feelings to flow unhindered as you journal.

SHARING GOD'S LOVE

This week, think of one woman who needs to grow in the knowledge of God's love—one who needs to believe that she is "fearfully and wonderfully made." Each day of the week, spend a few minutes in prayer asking God to help her see herself the way God sees her, that she would grow in the knowledge of God's love and, in turn, learn to love herself in healthy ways. If the opportunity arises, share God's love with her in a tangible way. Pay her a compliment, write her an encouraging note, sing a song to her, send her an e-card, or do what comes naturally for you.

You have now finished your second lesson. I pray that God has blessed your study time and that you are experiencing God in amazing ways! In lesson 3, "God's True Nature," you will learn about the character of God and heal any distorted images of God you have held.

God's True Nature   *Lesson 3*

YOU ARE AN AMAZING woman of God, created in the very image of God. As you gaze in the mirror each day, see the beauty of the Lord radiating from your countenance. How lovely you are—God's own special workmanship designed especially for God's pleasure and purpose. Is it not thrilling to know how much you mean to God? What powerful truths to assimilate! Assimilating such truths for survivors is a process, though; sometimes it is a lifelong process. Since the ravages of abuse attack the very soul of a child of God, it is commonplace to struggle not only with one's self-image, but also with one's image or perception of God. As mentioned in our previous lesson, our perpetrators (or caregivers, parents, significant others) act as mirrors—distorted mirrors—sending false messages about who we are as children of God. These distorted images not only affect the way we feel and think about ourselves, but they also affect the way we view God.

Now, add to these realities the fact that we also may have been mistreated, misunderstood, or misinformed in the church by a pastor or Christian leader who did not understand the dynamics of abuse and, unfortunately, helped reinforce our negative perceptions of God.

What do you really believe about God, the one whom you image? Is God loving and compassionate? Is God faithful to his promises? Is God trustworthy? Is God a just God? Does God desire intimacy with his people? And is God's desire for us to be in healthy, loving, intimate relationships with others?

What do you really believe about God? Record your thoughts on the lines below.

In this lesson, we will grapple with some of these important questions about God's nature and try to help heal our image of God. Before you begin, ask God to bless your time spent with him and to open your heart and mind as you study his word this week.

Before we delve into the Scriptures, please take a few moments and jot down some of your images or perceptions of God. How do you see God—not what the Bible says or what you have been taught, but how do you honestly image God? Many women that I have encouraged over the years in their journeys to healing and wholeness have held distorted views of God. Some have seen God as cold and distant; others have seen God as critical, stern, and abusive, like a taskmaster trying to make them jump through hoops to measure up. Others have seen God as detached, angry, and uncaring.[1] Some have seen God as an abandoner, one who abandons his people when they do not obey.[2] Others have seen God as unreliable and untrustworthy, and still others have imaged God as unfair.[3]

Can you relate to these images of God? Although I imagine you can relate, these images are anything but true. They are just that—merely false images of God, and they do not reflect God's true nature.

So who is God? What does the Bible say about God's true nature? Let us learn more accurately who God is. Oh, Lord, please bring revelation to our hearts and minds as we study your word.

In our first lesson, we learned that God loves us so much that he willingly gave up his only Son on our behalf. There is no greater love than this. Thus, we know that God is a loving God, for God is love. Let us review one Scripture passage about the deep love of God: Isaiah 43:1–4. We will also look at Deuteronomy 7:9, Psalm 12:6, Hebrews 6:13–15, Isaiah 61:1–4, Matthew 9:20–22, and Isaiah 54:1–7.

---

1. Sandra D. Wilson and Gary R. Collins, eds, *Counseling Adult Children of Alcoholics: Resources for Christian Counseling* (Dallas: Word, 1989), 95–100.

2. Steven R. Tracy, *Mending the Soul: Understanding and Healing* Abuse (Grand Rapids: Zondervan, 2005), 172–74.

3. Ibid.

LEARNING GOD'S TRUTH

Read Isaiah 43:1–4.

> ¹But now thus says the LORD, he who created you, O Jacob, he who formed you, O Israel: Do not fear, for I have redeemed you; I have called you by name, you are mine. ²When you pass through the waters, I will be with you; and through the rivers, they shall not overwhelm you; when you walk through fire you shall not be burned, and the flame shall not consume you. ³For I am the LORD your God, the Holy One of Israel, your Savior. I give Egypt as your ransom, Ethiopia and Seba in exchange for you. ⁴Because you are precious in my sight, and honored, and I love you, I give people in return for you, nations in exchange for your life.

No matter what we go through in life, what should be our reaction to fear according to this passage? (v. 1)

Read this passage through once or twice and write down everything that God says about you.

In the same way that God loves the nation of Israel, God loves you. God is even willing to give nations in exchange for you. God loves and accepts you as his covenant child; this is a reality. Spend a few minutes in prayer thanking God for his thoughts and feelings toward you.

Let us move on to understanding more clearly God's faithfulness. Although one of your images of God may be unreliable or untrustworthy, God is unswervingly faithful to you.

Please read Deuteronomy 7:9.

> Know therefore that the LORD your God is God, the faithful God who maintains covenant loyalty with those who love him and keep his commandments, to a thousand generations. . . ."

According to this passage, how does God show his faithfulness to you, his covenant child?

_____

_____

What is a covenant?

_____

How long does God maintain his covenant with you?

_____

What do you think "a thousand generations" represents? Explain.

_____

_____

God is a God of intimate relationships, and, from the beginning, he made promises to his beloved people. God calls us to live in a covenant relationship with him.

Please read Psalm 12:6 and Hebrews 6:13–15.

> The promises of the LORD are promises that are pure, silver refined in a furnace on the ground, purified seven times. (Psa 12:6)

What do you think it means that the Lord's promises are "like silver refined in a furnace?"

_____

_____

What does it mean for promises to be "purified seven times?"

_____

_____

> [13]When God made a promise to Abraham, because he had no one greater by whom to swear, he swore by himself, [14]saying, "I will surely bless you and multiply you." [15]And thus Abraham, having patiently endured, obtained the promise. (Heb 6:13–15)

To whom did God swear by when he made a promise to Abraham?

_____

Is there any greater name in heaven and on earth to swear by?

What was God's promise to Abraham?

Did God keep his promise to Abraham? (See v. 15) Explain.

While Abraham waited for the fulfillment of his promise, what action did he take?

What special promise(s) has God spoken to your heart?

If God's promise has not been realized, how might you respond to God while you await its fulfillment?

Write down God's promise to you and pray for patience and faithfulness while you await your heart's desire. How are you doing? Are you beginning to image God more accurately as a God of steadfast love and faithfulness, one who keeps his covenant to a thousand generations? I pray that you are. Let us now learn more about God as compassion.

Read Isaiah 61:1–4 and Matthew 9:20–22.

> [1]The spirit of the Lord God is upon me, because the Lord has anointed me; he has sent me to bring good news to the oppressed, to bind up the brokenhearted, to proclaim liberty to the captives, and release to the prisoners; [2]to proclaim the year of the Lord's favor, and the day of vengeance of our God; to comfort all who mourn; [3]to provide for those who mourn in Zion—to give them a

garland instead of ashes, the oil of gladness instead of mourning, the mantle of praise instead of a faint spirit. They will be called oaks of righteousness, the planting of the LORD, to display his glory. 4They shall build up the ancient ruins, they shall raise up the former devastations; they shall repair the ruined cities, the devastations of many generations. (Isa 61:1–4)

Isaiah 61:1–4 is a prophecy about Jesus, the coming Messiah. Can you imagine, Isaiah prophesied Jesus' coming and mission to the church two thousand years before his birth?

What was Jesus' mission to the church? (vv. 1–2)

_____

_____

What is the good news? Does the good news include binding up the brokenhearted? Explain.

_____

_____

What do you think it means "to bind up the brokenhearted"? How do you bind up one's (broken) heart?

_____

What is the imagery that comes to mind for you?

_____

_____

What does a garland symbolize (v. 3)?

_____

What is the difference between a garland and ashes?

_____

_____

Why exchange a garland for ashes?

_____

_____

What does the symbol of "oil of gladness" mean to you? What is it replacing?

_____

_____

Can you understand the depth of God's compassion for the brokenhearted?

_____

What does God's compassion look like for you? How does God show his compassion?

_____

_____

Can you think of another Scripture passage that demonstrates God's compassion? (See Matt 9:20.)

Share your thoughts and feelings.

Let us turn to Isaiah 54:1–17 and read it through. You may want to reread the passage as you seek to answer the questions.

> ¹Sing, O barren one who did not bear; burst into song and shout, you who have not been in labor! For the children of the desolate woman will be more than the children of her that is married, says the LORD. ²Enlarge the site of your tent, and let the curtains of your habitations be stretched out; do not hold back; lengthen your cords and strengthen your stakes. ³For you will spread out to the right and to the left, and your descendants will possess the nations and will settle the desolate towns. ⁴Do not fear, for you will not be ashamed; do not be discouraged, for you will not suffer disgrace; for you will forget the shame of your youth, and the disgrace of your widowhood you will remember no more. ⁵For your Maker is your husband, the LORD of hosts is his name; the Holy One of Israel is your Redeemer, the God of the whole earth he is called. ⁶For the LORD has called you like a wife forsaken and grieved in spirit, like the wife of a man's youth when she is cast off, says your God. ⁷For a brief moment I abandoned you, but with great compassion I will gather you. ⁸In overflowing wrath for a moment I hid my face from you, but with everlasting love I will have compassion on you, says the LORD, your Redeemer. ⁹This is like the days of Noah to me: Just as I swore that the waters of Noah would never again go over the earth, so I have sworn that I will not be angry with you and will not rebuke you. ¹⁰For the mountains may depart and the hills be removed, but my steadfast love shall not depart from you,

and my covenant of peace shall not be removed, says the LORD, who has compassion on you. ¹¹O afflicted one, storm-tossed, and not comforted, I am about to set your stones in antimony, and lay your foundations with sapphires. ¹²I will make your pinnacles of rubies, your gates of jewels, and all your wall of precious stones. ¹³All your children shall be taught by the LORD, and great shall be the prosperity of your children. ¹⁴In righteousness you shall be established; you shall be far from oppression, for you shall not fear; and from terror, for it shall not come near you. ¹⁵If anyone stirs up strife, it is not from me; whoever stirs up strife with you shall fall because of you. ¹⁶See it is I who have created the smith who blows the fire of coals, and produces a weapon fit for its purpose; I have also created the ravager to destroy. ¹⁷No weapon that is fashioned against you shall prosper, and you shall confute every tongue that rises against you in judgment. This is the heritage of the servants of the LORD and their vindication from me, says the LORD.

Share how this passage speaks to you. What can you relate to?

_____

_____

_____

_____

Although your suffering has been most painful, one day it will seem like "a brief moment" when you experience the depth of God's compassion for you as God gathers you into his intimate embrace.

Share your thoughts:

_____

_____

According to this passage, how is the Lord like a husband?

_____

Does this imagery comfort you? If so, share how it comforts you.

_____

According to this passage, does God desire intimacy or closeness with you? What words or phrases bring you to this conclusion?

_____

What would intimacy with God look like for you?

_____

_____

In this passage, what descriptions of God do you see?

_____

_____

Do you see the other attributes we have already studied (love, faithfulness)?

_____

_____

List the verses where you see these attributes recorded:

_____

_____

EXPERIENCING GOD

Please find a quiet, comfortable place to be alone with God. Close your eyes as you rest in God. Try to center in Christ, surrendering all distracting thoughts into God's care. Spend about ten minutes in silent prayer. Think of yourself as soaking in the presence of God. When you are finished, take five or ten minutes to journal any thoughts or feelings that came to you while you were praying. What was God saying to you? Did God reveal anything about his word to you while you were centering in him? If so, what did he impress on your heart and mind?

SHARING GOD'S LOVE

Think of an attribute of God that you most need to grow in (love, gentleness, kindness, patience, etc). Allow God to use you to share this attribute with another person. For example, be patient with someone in your life who ordinarily may drive you to act impatiently. Or, express God's love to someone who is not easy to love. Pray before you act and allow God to use you to bless his beloved child.

You are amazing, and you have done tremendous work! It's not easy reorienting your thinking about God's nature, but it is refreshing to know the truth and to be able to continue to grow in understanding who God is and who you are in relation to God. Lesson 4, "Expressing Your God-Given Emotions," will encourage you to learn to process your unwanted emotions in healthy, life-renewing ways. I pray that you will experience freedom in expressing and processing your emotions.

Expressing Your God-Given Emotions   *Lesson 4*

IN THIS LESSON, WE are going to talk about our God-given emotions and learn how to express them freely and positively. As survivors of abuse, we have felt a wide range of negative emotions, and, oftentimes, we have not possessed the tools to process them in healthy, constructive ways. Rather than trying to understand why we feel the way we do and what we can do to change things, we often numb out or repress these painful, confusing, and unwanted emotions. Unfortunately, we end up harming ourselves further.

However, the truth remains: God made us emotional beings, and this is a good thing! God gave us emotions as an indicator to help us understand what we are feeling and why, and to help us determine what we need so we can lovingly care for ourselves. Therefore, instead of allowing our emotions to overwhelm us and to cause us to self-destruct, we need to learn to express them in positive and life-renewing ways.

How many of you struggle on a regular basis with negative feelings such as guilt, shame, anger, depression, or rejection? Would it not be a wonderful thing to learn how to handle your feelings and emotions so that they do not continue to drain the energy and life out of you? After all, the Bible tells us that Jesus came not only to give us life, but he came to give us abundant life. And part of living life abundantly means to be free to feel our feelings—and not just the negative ones—and to be the women God created us to be.

So, I would like you to consider the following three questions:

1) Do you want to be emotionally whole?

2) Do you want to learn more about yourself in relationship to your emotions and learn to express them in healthy, constructive, and life-sustaining ways?

3) Do you want to be free to express your authentic self, whatever it is that you are feeling, so that you can be true to yourself and others and have the intimacy in your relationships that you have always longed for?

Do I hear a resounding "Yes" to all three? If so, go for it!

This is definitely possible with God's help and with a deeper self-understanding as emotional beings. Today, let us take a journey in the Bible and learn what God says about who we are as emotional beings and how we can embrace our feelings and emotions and constructively deal with them so that they become our friends and not enemies holding us captive. We will also learn how to change our thinking patterns and negative belief systems so we are not living with debilitating feelings and emotions, but more pleasant and enlivening ones instead. Before we move on to our Bible passages, let us first define the words "emotion" and "feeling."

According to Archibald Hart, who wrote *Unlocking the Mystery of Your Emotions* and served as dean of the graduate School of Psychology at Fuller Theological Seminary, feelings are a part of one's emotion. "They are the part of emotion that breaks through into our awareness. A feeling is the sensation or bodily state that accompanies the experience of the emotion. An emotion refers to the deeper, underlying state that stirs or agitates us, whether or not we are aware of it as feeling. The term emotion, therefore, refers to the state of our being. Feeling is how we experience that state."[1] Moreover, Dr. Hart believes that "People feel what they think and their emotions are the complete sum of all their thoughts."[2] What a profound truth for us to meditate on.

Please take a few moments to pray and ask God to give you insight into yourself and your emotions this week. Write your prayer on the lines below.

_____

_____

_____

_____

_____

_____

1. Archibald D. Hart, *Unlocking the Mystery of Your Emotions* (Dallas: Word, 1989), 14.

2. Ibid.

LEARNING GOD'S TRUTH

In lesson 4, we will study Daniel 5:6–12 and 1 Samuel 1:1–20.
Please turn now to the Book of Daniel and read Daniel 5:6–12.

> ⁶Then the king's face turned pale, and his thoughts terrified him.
> His limbs gave way, and his knees knocked together. ⁷The king
> cried aloud to bring in the enchanters, the Chaldeans, and the di-
> viners; and the king said to the wise men of Babylon, "Whoever can
> read this writing and tell me its interpretation shall be clothed in
> purple, have a chain of gold around his neck, and rank third in the
> kingdom." ⁸Then all the king's wise men came in, but they could
> not read the writing or tell the king the interpretation. ⁹Then King
> Belshazzar became greatly terrified and his face turned pale, and
> his lords were perplexed. ¹⁰The queen, when she heard the discus-
> sion of the king and his lords, came into the banqueting hall. The
> queen said, "O king, live forever! Do not let your thoughts terrify
> you or your face grow pale. ¹¹There is a man in your kingdom who
> is endowed with a spirit of the holy gods. In the days of your father
> he was found to have enlightenment, understanding, and wisdom
> like the wisdom of the gods. Your father, King Nebuchadnezzar,
> made him chief of the magicians, enchanters, Chaldeans, and di-
> viners, ¹²because an excellent spirit, knowledge, and understand-
> ing to interpret dreams, explain riddles, and solve problems were
> found in this Daniel, whom the king named Belteshazzar. Now let
> Daniel be called, and he will give the interpretation."

In this Bible passage, (v. 10) we see that King Belshazzar's wife was
warning him not to allow his thoughts to trouble or terrify him as a result
of the unpleasant news he had received. We understand from this how
easy it is to allow the thoughts in our minds and the beliefs in our hearts
to affect the way we feel. In this case, the king, having an unrepentant
heart, really had something to worry about as Daniel interpreted the writing on the wall (vv. 22–23). However, oftentimes, even though we are
beloved children of God, instead of trusting that God is going to take care
of us, we worry and fret needlessly, causing many unpleasant feelings.

Take a few moments and think of a time recently when you were
feeling good, and then your emotions suddenly changed for the worse.
What happened to effect this change? Record the sequence of events that
precipitated the change.

_____

_____

_____

It is true that our thoughts and our negative beliefs affect our emotions.

I remember when I was newly married, and I was going through major inner healing, how easy it was for me to fly off the handle at my husband because of my thinking and negative beliefs. For example, I would expect my husband to come home at a certain time from work, and when he would stroll through the door three hours late, I would feel hurt and angry. While I was patiently waiting for him to come home, my mind was working overtime creating all kinds of scenarios. I was imagining that he was with another woman or that he was doing something behind my back. At the time, I was also reminded of what my mother went through when she used to sit and wait for my father to come home from work—and he was always late. So, in this case, both my thoughts and my beliefs about marriage affected the way I felt. In addition, what I felt was hurt, disappointment, rejection, anger, and resentment. Now, before I discuss what I did to change my thinking and beliefs so that I could live a more peaceful and fruitful existence, we will next look at the story of Hannah in 1 Samuel 1:1–20.

> ¹There was a certain man of Ramathaim, a Zuphite from the hill country of Ephraim, whose name was Elkanah son of Jeroham son of Elihu son of Tohu son of Zuph, an Ephraimite. ²He had two wives; the name of the one was Hannah, and the name of the other Peninnah. Peninnah had children, but Hannah had no children. ³Now this man used to go up year by year from his town to worship and to sacrifice to the LORD of hosts at Shiloh, where the two sons of Eli, Hophni and Phinehas, were priests of the LORD. ⁴On the day when Elkanah sacrificed, he would give portions to his wife Peninnah and to all her sons and daughters; ⁵but to Hannah he gave a double portion, because he loved her, though the LORD had closed her womb. ⁶Her rival used to provoke her severely, to irritate her, because the LORD had closed her womb. ⁷So it went on year by year; as often as she went up to the house of the LORD, she used to provoke her. Therefore Hannah wept and would not eat. ⁸Her husband Elkanah said to her, "Hannah, why do you weep? Why do you not eat? Why is your heart sad? Am I not more to you than ten sons?" ⁹After they had eaten and drunk at Shiloh, Hannah rose and presented herself before the LORD. Now Eli the priest was sitting on the seat beside the doorpost of the temple of the LORD. ¹⁰She was deeply distressed and prayed to the LORD, and wept bitterly. ¹¹She made this vow: "O LORD of hosts, if only

you will look on the misery of your servant, and remember me, and not forget your servant, but will give to your servant a male child, then I will set him before you as a nazirite until the day of his death. He shall drink neither wine nor intoxicants, and no razor shall touch his head." ¹²As she continued praying before the LORD, Eli observed her mouth. ¹³Hannah was praying silently; only her lips moved, but her voice was not heard; therefore Eli thought she was drunk. ¹⁴So Eli said to her, "How long will you make a drunken spectacle of yourself? Put away your wine." ¹⁵But Hannah answered, "No, my lord, I am a woman deeply troubled; I have drunk neither wine nor strong drink, but I have been pouring out my soul before the LORD. ¹⁶Do not regard your servant as a worthless woman, for I have been speaking out of my great anxiety and vexation all this time." ¹⁷Then Eli answered, "Go in peace; the God of Israel grant the petition you have made to him." ¹⁸And she said, "Let your servant find favor in your sight." Then the woman went to her quarters, ate and drank with her husband, and her countenance was sad no longer. ¹⁹They rose early in the morning and worshiped before the LORD; then they went back to their house at Ramah. Elkanah knew his wife Hannah, and the LORD remembered her. ²⁰In due time Hannah conceived and bore a son. She named him Samuel, for she said, "I have asked him of the LORD."

Describe what Hannah may have been feeling (vv. 5–10).

_____

_____

Do you think that Hannah was depressed?

_____

What words in this passage lead you to believe that she was depressed?

_____

_____

When do you think that Hannah's sad feelings over her barrenness changed: before or after she gave birth to Samuel?

_____

_____

Share in your own words what you think happened to change her feelings.

_____

_____

How do you think that God felt about Hannah's sadness and feelings of rejection? Do you think God cared about Hannah's feelings?

_____

_____

If so, then why do you think that Hannah had to wait so long to have a child?

_____

_____

Hannah was special to God. In fact, Hannah was so special that God had a unique plan and purpose for her life. I believe with all my heart that God cared deeply over the way Hannah felt. Though her suffering endured for years, did God forget her? No, God never forgets his beloved.

This lesson will teach you how to get in touch with your true feelings and emotions and how to process them in healthy ways so that they do not overwhelm you or control you. Although Hannah may have felt abandoned by God, he knew the plans he had for her. Hannah was called upon by God to intercede, not only for a son, but for an entire nation. She was faithful to God and he blessed her beyond her highest expectations and prayers. He did not forget or neglect her. In God's perfect timing, Hannah became pregnant. And we know that Hannah believed God before she conceived, because her countenance changed (v. 18). She was joyful once more because she knew beyond any doubt that God had heard her prayer and she rejoiced immeasurably in God's faithfulness and unconditional love.

Do you believe that God cares about you and your feelings just as he cared for Hannah's? Explain.

_____

_____

So, now that we know that our thoughts and beliefs affect our emotions, and that God does indeed care how we feel, how do we change our thinking and beliefs so that we can experience more pleasant and desirable emotions? Now, of course, we are not perfect and will not always be able to feel good about everything in our lives, yet it is possible to experience a more peaceful and emotionally stable life.

The first thing that I believe you can do when you are feeling a negative emotion is to take a few moments and ask yourself, "What am I feeling, and why?" Get in touch with the emotion, feel it, and try to understand what is going on within you. (And if you have time, you can monitor your emotions by keeping a journal of what you are feeling and why.) For instance, if you are feeling guilty over some event, discern whether this guilt is founded or not. In other words, is it false or true guilt? If your conscience has a reason to feel guilty, then take this problem to God and repent of whatever it is that is causing you the guilt feeling and receive God's forgiveness. If you determine that your guilt is unfounded, that you really did not do anything wrong, then ask God to relieve you of this inappropriate response to the guilt. If you continue to struggle with this, please talk to a friend or a trusted counselor about the problem. Remember, God wants you to be healthy in your emotions.

Take a few moments and think about a recent negative emotion that you felt. Name the emotion. What were you feeling? Why were you feeling that way? Share what comes.

A second and very important thing you can do to be free of unwanted emotions is to learn to take control of them—do not allow them to control you. And how do you do this? As James Allen says, "A noble and Godlike character is not a thing of favor or chance, but is the natural result of continued effort in right thinking. . . . [S]he is the maker of her character . . . if she will watch, control, and alter her thoughts, tracing their effects upon herself, upon others, and upon her life circumstances."[3]

In addition, I would add that the Holy Spirit changes us (and our thinking). As we surrender our thoughts to God, we will continuously be transformed in our thinking. Therefore, you can change your emotions if you watch, control, and alter your thoughts, of course, with the help of the Holy Spirit. For example, how did I change my thinking about my husband coming home late, and how did this affect my emotions and ultimately my marriage?

---

3. James Allen, *As a Man Thinketh* (Old Tappan, N.J.: Fleming H. Revell, 1977), quoted in Archibald D. Hart, *Unlocking the Mystery of Your Emotions* (Dallas: Word Publishing, 1989), 29.

Watch—I began to pay attention to my thinking processes. I noticed when my mind was becoming suspicious and when I was feeling insecure and was getting ready to explode in anger when my husband walked through the door late.

Control—I got in touch with the underlying feelings of mistrust, fear of abandonment, and insecurity, and then I began to turn the situation over to God. I asked God to help me to trust him even if I still did not fully trust my husband. As my trust in God began to increase, I stopped worrying about my husband's lateness. If he was late, he was late, and I did not expect that he would necessarily be home on time every night. I grew so much in my trust of God that I knew that God would never let me down even if my husband did. I knew that God loved me and that God would see me through. Even if my husband proved to be unfaithful (as a worst-case scenario), God would continue to be faithful to me.

Alter—As my thoughts changed gradually, I became much calmer, more peaceful, and more emotionally stable—a much easier person to live with. My security is rooted in God and not in another human being. This new way of thinking not only changed my life for the better, but my husband eventually came to trust in Christ because he saw such a dramatic difference in my reactions and behavior. Changing my thinking in a few areas affected the way I began to react and respond emotionally to many other situations. Of course, I am continuously being transformed in my mind and heart as I will never arrive, but I am thankful for what God has done already in my life.

A third thing that you can do if you are struggling with deep-seated emotions, such as shame over some behavior, is to try to get at the root of the issue. This might mean that you engage a minister, a friend, a counselor, or even a small group experience to help with this search. Oftentimes, if a person continuously feels a deep sense of shame, underlying the shame could be a fear of abandonment or some abusive event that precipitated this. God wants you healed from the inside out, and, at times, you have to travel back into the past to understand why you feel the way you do or why you behave the way you do. This takes time, for healing is a process. And, if you truly desire wholeness, I firmly believe that God will bring about this God-given desire. Often, getting to the root of an issue requires educating yourself by reading excellent books related to the topics you are dealing with. The best counseling is bringing awareness to you. Incidentally, the book by Dr. Hart, *Unlocking the Mystery of Your Emotions,* is one of the best books I have ever read on learning to deal with emotions in healthy ways. Another great book to help foster emotional and spiritual growth is the book *Unbound* by Neal Lozano. It is, by far, the best book I have read and practiced that helps facilitate inner healing and deliverance in God's children. It is biblically sound and theologically well balanced, and it offers a practical and loving approach to healing and deliverance.

A fourth thing, but probably the most important thing, that you can do is to continue to be faithful to God in your spiritual disciplines: Bible study, devotions, prayer, quiet, and solitude. This is crucial if you want to live in emotional freedom. Practicing the spiritual disciplines will bring about deep healing and cause you to mature in the fruit of the Holy Spirit. And, in doing so, you will grow in intimacy with God and learn to hear God's voice for direction in your life and ministry. God loves it when we spend time with him. He wants to heal your broken heart and rid you of unpleasant and irritating emotions. Come and sit at the feet of your Beloved and learn more about his unconditional love and acceptance of you.

EXPERIENCING GOD

Choose one of the following two exercises:

Zephaniah 3:17–20

Sit in a safe, quiet, and comfortable place with God. Pray in silence for five minutes. Then, ask God to show you how you see yourself. Journal what comes to your mind. Ask God to help you to see yourself the way God sees you. Remember, your thoughts affect the way you feel. Then take a few minutes and meditate on Zephaniah 3:17–20. Read this passage through slowly once and pay attention to any word or phrase that speaks to you. What is God saying to you? How does this make you feel? What feelings does this passage evoke? Read the passage a second time and respond to God by thanking God for who he created you to be. Journal your experience; write whatever comes.

Process a Negative Emotion

Take time to process your emotions. Think of a recent negative emotion you felt. What do you think was the root of this negative emotion? Share what comes to you. What were you thinking? How could you change your thinking to feel differently? Ask the Holy Spirit to guide you.

You have done great work today on working through the process of understanding your emotions and trying to pay attention to any wrong thinking that contributes to your unwanted feelings and emotions.

End this lesson by taking five or ten minutes and soak in the love of God. Sit quietly before the Lord and allow him to minister to you. What came up for you, or what did you sense God saying to you?

SHARING GOD'S LOVE

Think about someone this week who you know struggles with expressing his or her God-given emotions. Either pray for him or her to be able to express emotions more freely and handle the negative emotions more constructively, or talk to the person about what you have been learning. Perhaps this will enable that person to begin to live more freely in the area of emotions.

Bravo! Another lesson is completed. You are doing wonderfully as you process and work through some painful emotions and other issues. May God give you the courage and strength to keep persevering in the faith as you pursue healing and wholeness. In lesson 5, "Living in Freedom," you will learn more about what it means that Christ came to set captives free and wants you to live life abundantly! I pray that you will accept your freedom in Christ and live the rich, abundant life that Christ died for you to have!

Living in Freedom

I N THE LAST LESSON, we learned how to express and process our human emotions in life-renewing ways. It is surely a freeing experience when we can do this. However, living and experiencing true freedom in Christ includes more than an honest expression of our emotions and feelings. What does it truly mean to live freely in Christ? How often do you hear others say, "I want to be free in Christ. Oh, Lord set me free." I am sure you have also longed for, prayed about, and shared your desire for freedom. Well, God desires freedom for you more than you do—more than you can imagine! After all, for what purpose did Christ die? What was Christ's mission on earth? Does not the Bible tell us that Christ came "to set the captives free" (Isa 61:1)?

This week, we are going to learn what it means to live in freedom in Christ. If you in any way desire to experience a greater measure of freedom in Christ, read on. You will learn what it means to accept this freedom and what you can do to help facilitate freedom in your own life and the lives of others so that you can fulfill your God-given destiny in Christ Jesus.

For this lesson, we will read Luke 4:15–19; Exodus 3:7–9, 16–17; Psalm 103:6; John 8:31–32; 1 Thessalonians 5:16–18; Matthew 6:9–14, 14:23; Mark 6:46; Luke 6:12; and Deuteronomy 5:9–10.

Pray and ask the Lord to lead you and guide you as you study his word this week, and to allow you to experience a greater measure of freedom in your life so that you will be bubbling over with an unspeakable joy and zest for living unlike anything you have ever experienced before. Write your prayer on the lines below:

_____

_____

LEARNING GOD'S TRUTH

Read Luke 4:15–19.

> [15]He began to teach in their synagogues and was praised by everyone. [16]When he came to Nazareth, where he had been brought up, he went to the synagogue on the sabbath day, as was his custom. He stood up to read, [17]and the scroll of the prophet Isaiah was given to him. He unrolled the scroll and found the place where it was written: [18]"The Spirit of the Lord is upon me, because he has anointed me to bring good news to the poor. He has sent me to proclaim release to the captives and recovery of sight to the blind, to let the oppressed go free, [19]to proclaim the year of the Lord's favor."

In lesson 3, we read Isaiah 61:1–4, and, now in this passage in Luke, we see the fulfillment of this prophecy in Jesus' life. Absolutely amazing, is it not?

What is Jesus' mission to the church (vv. 18–19)?

_____

_____

How do you see God's compassion toward his people in relation to Jesus' mission?

_____

_____

What do you believe it means, "He has sent me to proclaim release to the captives"?

_____

_____

In what ways have you felt captive (or imprisoned)?

_____

_____

In what ways would you like to experience greater freedom? Write down whatever comes to you.

_____

_____

_____

What does the word "oppressed" mean in this context?

_____

The root word for "oppress" in Hebrew (Isa 61) means to "force one to submit" or to "inflict undue pain."[1] God does not want his children to live this way. He wants to release them from unhealthy ties that keep people in unnecessary bondage. Sometimes, it takes learning to set healthy boundaries and learning to care lovingly for yourself.

Read Exodus 3:7–9, 16–17 and Psalm 103:6.

> [7]Then the Lord said, I have observed the misery of my people who are in Egypt; I have heard their cry on account of their taskmasters. Indeed, I know their sufferings, [8]and I have come down to deliver them from the Egyptians, and to bring them up out of that land to a good and broad land, a land flowing with milk and honey, to the country of the Canaanites, the Hittites, the Amorites, the Perizzites, the Hivites, and the Jebusites. [9]The cry of the Israelites has now come to me; I have also seen how the Egyptians oppress them. . . . [16]Go and assemble the elders of Israel, and say to them, "The Lord, the God of your ancestors, the God of Abraham, of Isaac, and of Jacob, has appeared to me, saying: I have given heed to you and to what has been done to you in Egypt. [17]I declare that I will bring you up out of the misery of Egypt, to the land of the Canaanites, the Hittites, the Amorites, the Perizzites, the Hivites, and the Jebusites, a land flowing with milk and honey." (Exod 3:7–9, 16–17)

> The LORD works vindication and justice for all who are oppressed. (Psa 103:6)

Can you identify in any way with the Israelites' enslavement or heavy burden of oppression? (See Exod 1:8–14) Share your heart.

_____

_____

_____

How did God act to free his people?

_____

_____

1. Harris, R. L., and G. L. Archer, Jr., eds., *Theological Wordbook of the Old Testament*, n.p., BibleWorks. Version 6.0.005y, 2003.

Do you believe that God understands your suffering and wants to put an end to it?

_____

What is "a good and broad place, a land flowing with milk and honey"? (Exod 3:17)

_____

_____

What would this look like or feel like for you? What is your heart's desire?

_____

_____

What does "a broad place, a land flowing with milk and honey" have to do with freedom?

_____

_____

When we read that Jesus "came to set the captives free," this means that Jesus lovingly and sacrificially gave his life to release you from sin (including sins perpetrated against you) and any kind of unhealthy bondage or oppression so that you can thrive in being the woman God created you to be. Since all things are possible with God, then God desires to bring you your heart's desire.

Take a moment to pray and reflect on your deepest desire.

God does not want his people living in oppressive conditions. God is loving and just. God will indeed act, but sometimes God needs you to act along with him. You can act by learning to set healthy boundaries and limits for what you will tolerate.

God's people should never tolerate abuse, and action must be taken to assure one's freedom. You must do everything you can to be free from any kind of unhealthy bondage or oppression. This is never God's will for your life! Sometimes, this means using tough love with a loved one, or seeking help from a trusted friend, an understanding pastor, or a professional counselor. At times, this requires taking drastic measures, such as separating from an abusive spouse or loved one. Divorce may be necessary if the abuse continues. Each case is unique. This is where you can really benefit from an understanding pastor or a professional, compassionate, and experienced counselor.

God desires for you to live life abundantly and to enjoy the freedom from oppression and sin (including sins against you) for which he died. God desires for you to be the woman of God that he created you to be, and this means using all your gifts and talents for his glory. God wants you to experience such freedom that you are able to enjoy the rich, abundant life that he came to give you. With God, since heaven is the limit, you should be free to be all that God intended you to be—free to love (including loving yourself), dance, sing, and laugh; free to create through the arts; free to express your honest and true emotions and feelings; and free to know (and experience) how deeply you are loved by God—that you are indeed accepted in the Beloved. Do not wait; you have missed so much already. Go forth into your God-given destiny and do not let anything or anyone hold you back. Be free in Christ. Live free.

Maintaining Our Freedom through Spiritual Disciplines

Read John 8:31–32.

> 31Then Jesus said to the Jews who had believed in him, "If you continue in my word, you are truly my disciples; 32and you will know the truth, and the truth will make you free."

How will you know the truth?

_____

What makes you free?

_____

Why is it important to read the word every day?

_____
_____

Read 1 Thessalonians 5:15–18 and Matthew 6:9–14.

15See that none of you repays evil for evil, but always seek to do good to one another and to all. 16Rejoice always, 17pray without ceasing, 18give thanks in all circumstances; for this is the will of God in Christ Jesus for you. (1 Thess 5:15–18)

How often shall we pray? (v. 17) _____

What is God's will for us (v. 18)? _____

9Pray then in this way: Our Father in heaven, hallowed be your name. 10Your kingdom come. Your will be done, on earth as it is in heaven. 11Give us this day our daily bread. 12And forgive us our debts, as we also have forgiven our debtors. 13And do not bring us to the time of trial, but rescue us from the evil one. 14For if you forgive others their trespasses, your heavenly Father will also forgive you. (Matt 6:9–14)

Should forgiveness be a part of our daily prayer life?

_____

How shall we ask God to "forgive us our sins"? (v. 12)

_____

_____

What does God do when we forgive others (v. 14)?

_____

How important is forgiveness in experiencing freedom? Explain.

_____

_____

_____

When I first led support groups for survivors of abuse, I was told not to force the issue of forgiveness, since forgiveness is a process. First, we must realize how our perpetrator's sin (and victimization) has harmed and damaged us and how it has affected our lives before we attempt to forgive. In other words, we must understand what we are actually forgiving. Second, we can forgive even if our "debtor" has never taken ownership for his or her sin—even if that person never admits or confesses the wrongdoing. Third, releasing our "debtor" is in no way letting a perpetrator off the hook or exonerating him or her from any retribution. What that person did was sinfully wrong, and the Lord will judge him or her for the wrongdoing. (Please read chapter 10 of *Mending the Soul*—one of the best chapters I have ever read on the topic of forgiveness.)[2]

Forgiveness should most definitely be a part of our daily prayer life. It is so freeing when we are able, through the grace and power of the Holy Spirit, to forgive someone from the heart. When I was finally able to forgive one of my perpetrators, it was as if someone removed ten thousand pounds from my back.

We learned that one crucial spiritual discipline is daily Bible reading. What is another important discipline for maintaining our freedom?

Read Matthew 14:23, Mark 6:46, and Luke 6:12.

> And after he had dismissed the crowds, he went up the mountain by himself to pray. When evening came, he was there alone. (Matt 14:23)

> After saying farewell to them, he went up on the mountain to pray. (Mark 6:46)

> Now during those days he went out to the mountain to pray; and he spent the night in prayer to God. (Luke 6:12)

What was Jesus going to do in each situation?

_____

_____

Why did Jesus choose to be alone with the Father rather than be with the crowds?

_____

_____

What was Jesus seeking in his alone time?

_____

_____

What do you seek when you spend time alone with God?

_____

_____

_____

2. Steven R. Tracy, *Mending the Soul: Understanding and Healing* Abuse (Grand Rapids: Zondervan, 2005).

Jesus is God in the flesh, and if anyone knew the will of God, it was Jesus. But Jesus, the second person of the Trinity, always chose to move away from the crowds in order to be alone with the Father to pray.

What should we learn from Jesus' example?

_____

_____

The first spiritual discipline is reading God's word, and the second is prayer.

What is the third spiritual discipline that we should practice, using Jesus as our example?

_____

I imagine you are wondering what this practice has to do with freedom in Christ. How will this practice bring more freedom to your life? How will practicing solitude help you to maintain your freedom? Write down your thoughts, reflections, and ideas (for example, hearing God's voice better, knowing God's will for our lives, developing intimacy, learning to rest and be rather than do, or have more to give others when we meet with Jesus).

Read Deuteronomy 5:9–10.

> 9You shall not bow down to them or worship them; for I the LORD your God am a jealous God, punishing children for the iniquity of parents, to the third and fourth generation of those who reject me, 10but showing steadfast love to the thousandth generation of those who love me and keep my commandments.

How do you feel about this passage?

_____

_____

What do you think it means?

_____

_____

Moses is reciting the Ten Commandments to Israel, reminding them of their covenant relationship to God (see v. 10). God shows steadfast love to you to the thousandth generation—God is amazingly faithful to his own. But, sometimes our lives are very difficult and painful because of our parents' and grandparents' sins. Oftentimes, I have felt that I was paying the price for the sins of my family, the generational curses. It is common to unconsciously bond with what is familiar and end up repeating unhealthy family patterns.

Shortly after a close friend of mine was married, she said that she woke up one day and discovered that she was living out her parents' unhealthy nightmare of a marriage. She realized that she was acting like her mother and that she had chosen a husband who behaved like her father. It was as if she were reenacting her parents' unhealthy marriage (the unconscious choice we make to marry someone). It dawned on her as a new Christian that she did not want to live this way for the rest of her life. She began working on her own issues and was determined to break the curse of the generations over her life. It was a slow healing process, but what she eventually learned was that she needed to incorporate some healthy Christian practices into her daily life if she wanted to experience a normal healthy life and maintain her freedom in Christ.

EXPERIENCING GOD

Jesus is the Master Creator (Gen 1). He created you and made you unique and precious in his eyes. Since you are created in God's image, you, too, have the ability to create through various art forms. Take a block of time to create something that symbolizes your freedom or the freedom you desire. Begin by spending a few minutes in silence and then ask God to guide your hands and your heart. Write a poem or a story. Compose a song. Paint or draw a picture. Take a photo. Sculpt a piece of clay. Sew or knit a piece of fabric. Create whatever comes, allowing the Spirit to lead you giving you fresh new ideas.

SHARING GOD'S LOVE

Write a letter or call someone in your family and share what God is teaching you, or do an act of kindness for that person as an expression of God's love for you and for them.

I trust that you learned a great deal more about living freely in Christ. Go for it! Do what you need to do to continue to seek freedom from whatever is hindering you. Your freedom was purchased through the blood of Christ. Break free and become the person God desires for you to be!

Well, you have one more lesson, "Discovering Your Call," and my prayer is that you will find meaning and purpose in all that you have gone through, and that you will most definitely fulfill your God-given destiny in Christ. You are an amazing child of God, and God has great plans to prosper you as you use your gifts and talents to glorify God's name.

Discovering Your Call

Lesson 6

IN THE LAST LESSON, we learned that God desires for us to live in freedom in Christ and to be the women God created us to be. This includes using all our gifts and abilities to serve God. No matter what we endure in life, no matter how difficult or painful our circumstances, one thing is certain: God will use all our suffering to bring glory to his name. Nothing we go through need be without meaning and purpose. When we find meaning and purpose in our suffering, it offers great hope and encouragement to continue on the journey.

Have you ever wondered, "What is the meaning and purpose of all I have gone through in this life? And how could God possibly use me or my life circumstances to bring glory to his name?" Discovering your meaning and purpose in life has a lot to do with discovering your call. God has created you in his own image, and, in doing so, he has uniquely gifted you unlike anyone else. Let us take time this week to discover your unique calling in Christ.

Please take a few moments to pray and ask God to show you your unique gifts and calling so that you can understand yourself better and use all that God created you to be to bring glory and honor to his name.

Write your prayer on the lines below.

LEARNING GOD'S TRUTH

For lesson 6, we will read Acts 17:28; 1 Corinthians 12:4–9; Ephesians 2:10, 4:11–13; Proverbs 3:5–6; Philippians 2:12–13; and Matthew 22:37–39.

God created you with unique gifts in order to fulfill God's purposes for your life.

Read Acts 17:28; 1 Corinthians 12:4–9; and Ephesians 2:10, 4:11–18.

> For in him we live and move and have our being; as even some of your own poets have said, "For we too are his offspring." (Acts 17:28)

> 4Now there are varieties of gifts, but the same Spirit; 5and there are varieties of services, but the same Lord; 6and there are varieties of activities, but it is the same God who activates all of them in everyone. 7To each is given the manifestation of the Spirit for the common good. 8To one is given through the Spirit the utterance of wisdom, and to another the utterance of knowledge according to the same Spirit, 9to another faith by the same Spirit, to another gifts of healing by the one Spirit. (1 Cor 12:4–9)

> For we are what he has made us, created in Christ Jesus for good works, which God prepared beforehand to be our way of life. (Eph 2:10)

> 11The gifts he gave were that some would be apostles, some prophets, some evangelists, some pastors and teachers, 12to equip the saints for the work of ministry, for building up the body of Christ, 13until all of us come to the unity of the faith and of the knowledge of the Son of God, to maturity, to the measure of the full stature of Christ. (Eph 4:11–13)

Fill in the blanks (Acts 17:28). In God we ＿＿＿＿＿＿＿＿＿ and ＿＿＿＿＿＿＿＿＿ and ＿＿＿＿＿＿＿＿＿.

What does this mean to you? Share your thoughts.

＿＿＿＿＿＿＿＿＿＿＿＿＿＿＿＿＿＿＿＿＿＿＿＿＿＿＿＿＿＿＿＿

＿＿＿＿＿＿＿＿＿＿＿＿＿＿＿＿＿＿＿＿＿＿＿＿＿＿＿＿＿＿＿＿

＿＿＿＿＿＿＿＿＿＿＿＿＿＿＿＿＿＿＿＿＿＿＿＿＿＿＿＿＿＿＿＿

Of all the spiritual gifts that Paul mentions, which gifts do you have (1 Cor 12)? How are you using them, or how do you see yourself using them in the future?

_____

_____

Why do we have gifts? (Eph 4:12–13)?

_____

Take a few moments to jot down what you think God may have uniquely created you to do.

_____

_____

_____

Think about the most painful thing you have had to experience in your life. How could God use your suffering to bring good out of this evil? What might he ask you to do? What would you like to do? Share anything that comes to your mind; try not to limit yourself or God. God is a big God, and capable of using you beyond your highest prayers and expectations.

God will empower you through his Spirit to use your gifts as you follow his way.

Read Proverbs 3:5–6, Philippians 2:12–13, and Matthew 22:37–39.

> 5Trust in the Lord with all your heart, and do not rely on your own insight. 6In all your ways acknowledge him, and he will make straight your paths. (Prov 3:5–6)

> 12Work out your salvation with fear and trembling, 13for it is God who is at work in you, enabling you both to will and to work for his good pleasure. (Phil 2:12–13)

> 37He said to him, "'You shall love the Lord your God with all your heart, and with all your soul, and with all your mind.' 38This is the greatest and first commandment. 39And a second is like it: 'You shall love your neighbor as yourself.'" (Matt 22:37–39)

Why do you think we are told, "Do not rely on your own insight" (Prov 3:5)? _____

Fill in the blank: Trust in the Lord _____ (Prov 3:5a). What does this mean to you?

_____

_____

What are "straight paths"? (Prov 3:6)

_____

How are you enabled to do God's work? (Phil 2:13)

_____

What are you enabled to do? Why?

_____

_____

What are the two greatest commandments (Matt 22:37–39)?

_____

_____

How do these commandments fit with your calling?

_____

_____

If you could do anything your heart desires, what would it be?

_____

_____

_____

_____

Remember, you can do all things through Christ who strengthens you (Phil 4:13).

Discovering Your Gifts and Calling

According to Arthur Miller in his book *The Power of Uniqueness: How to Become Who You Really Are,* "Giftedness is who we are by nature. It is what makes us us. It is the way we were designed to function, and therefore the way we actually do function best and with the greatest delight . . .

Giftedness is more than a mere inventory of talents. It is the lifeblood of a person, the song that her heart longs to sing, the race that her legs long to run."[1] God has uniquely gifted you and desires you use all your gifts to fulfill your destiny![2] You can see how freeing this is to discover who you are and to be able to implement your gifts in your life's work.

In seeking to discover your God-given call, you must ask yourself, "What do I do well and what gives me pleasure?"[3] God wants you to enjoy using your gifts as you serve him with your life's work. And, no matter what pain or suffering you have experienced, there is nothing that can keep you from realizing God's call and destiny for your life. God created you with your own unique mapping (pattern of doing things) and motivation, and no life circumstance can repress your natural and innate giftedness.[4] You are who you are, by God's design.

EXPERIENCING GOD

Take time this week to write about and reflect upon your gifts and God's unique call on your life. As you reflect on your childhood and adulthood, think about your accomplishments and record the ones that you most enjoyed doing and did well.[5] Write down as many accomplishments as come to your mind, and include any pertinent details. Then, when you have made a list of accomplishments, make a list of the four that you enjoyed the most. Examine these four in detail and see what patterns emerge. What are the similarities in each? Is there a similar motivation pattern or passion? What do you notice about yourself? Do you notice anything different about yourself than you have ever noticed before?

Take as long as you need this week to work on this exercise, since it will help you discover your call. Ask the Lord to guide you and give you insight into your own unique mapping. Understand that your achievements are not necessarily successes; they are those activities that gave you

---

1. Arthur F. Miller, *The Power of Uniqueness: How to Become Who You Really Are* (Grand Rapids: Zondervan, 1999), 32, 39.

2. Ibid., 120.

3. Ibid., 37.

4. Ibid., 78.

5. See Appendix D, entitled "Discovering Your Design: A Step-by-Step Guide," in *The Power of Uniqueness* for additional information on this process.

passion and motivated you.[6] You can share your earliest memories; you can begin by sharing from your early childhood and into adulthood.

For example, let me share one of my early achievements and insights about my own uniqueness.

I enjoyed working at The Rental Company when I was in my twenties. I had my own space and office; no one told me what to do and when to do it. I set my own schedule. I was self-motivated. I arranged the office and hired the people I needed. I had the opportunity to meet all kinds of people, from all walks of life. I came to know their personal stories and, at times, even offered them spiritual and emotional help. I loved finding deals for people—great quality apartments for low rents. I enjoyed working with landlords and helping them find good tenants; this made them happy. I enjoyed matching the tenant with the apartment. I did not make a great deal of money, but this was not a priority for me. I felt good when I helped a person find a good deal—a great apartment for a reasonable rent—and when the landlord found a quality tenant. In assessing this achievement, I discovered that helping and serving are what I enjoyed the most and did well. But, I also needed space without anyone controlling me or telling me what to do, since I am an independent self-starter. I work well on my own, but I work more diligently and effectively when left alone. (For numerous examples, and for greater details in understanding your own unique patterns and giftedness, consult *The Power of Uniqueness*.)[7]

Sharing God's Love

Based on what you learned about yourself and your unique pattern and gifts, write three goals that will allow you to use your gifts. Begin working on accomplishing one of these goals this week.

1) _____

2) _____

3) _____

6. Ibid., 224.

7. Ibid.

Action Point for this week:

_____

_____

_____

Well, you have done it! You have completed all six lessons of the study *Accepted in the Beloved*. I pray that you have learned a great deal from each of the six lessons and that you are continuing to grow in the amazing unconditional love and acceptance of God. You are accepted in the Beloved.

Please take a few moments to jot down some important things you have learned from the six lessons. Journal or reflect upon anything new you have learned and the things that you still need to work on. Healing from abuse is a process, and it takes time to receive the healing that God desires for you. Please be patient and loving with yourself. And know that no matter what you are going through, or what you will go through in the future, that you are a precious child of the most high God, and you are indeed accepted in the Beloved!

Closing Prayer

Oh Lord, help me know *love*. I pray that I will continue to grow in the breadth, depth, height, and length of your love, and to know the love of Christ that surpasses knowledge, so that I may be filled with all the fullness of Christ. May I accomplish more with my life than my greatest expectations, prayers, and dreams (Eph 3:18–20 paraphrased). To God be the glory! Amen.

Made in the USA
San Bernardino, CA
22 March 2015